Where Roads May Lead

G.W. SCOTT

This is a second edition printing of *Where Roads May Lead*. Original copyright ©2012 G.W. Scott. All rights reserved.

Knoxville, Tennessee

Scriptures marked KJV are taken from the KING JAMES VERSION (KJV): KING JAMES VERSION, public domain.

Scripture quotations marked (NEB) are taken from The New English Bible, © 1970 by Oxford University Press and Cambridge University Press, printed in The United States of America.

Scriptures marked NKJV are taken from the NEW KING JAMES VERSION (NKJV): Scripture taken from the NEW KING JAMES VERSION®. Copyright© 1982 by Thomas Nelson, Inc. Used by permission. All rights reserved.

New Revised Standard Version Bible, copyright 1989, Division of Christian Education of the National Council of the Churches of Christ in the United States of America. Used by permission. All rights reserved.

No part of this book may be reproduced, stored in a retrieval system, or transmitted by any means without the written permission of the author.

First published by CrossBooks 02/2/2012
ISBN: 978-1-4627-1370-7
ISBN: 978-1-4627-1371-4
ISBN: 978-1-4627-1369-1
Second edition ISBN: 978-1-970037-51-7

Cover image is creative common use: http://i.stack.imgur.com/4rce5.jpg

Web links may have changed since publishing of the first edition and may no longer be valid. The views expressed in this work are solely those of the author and do not necessarily reflect the views of the publisher, and the publisher hereby disclaims any responsibility for them.

Printed in The United States of America

ACKNOWLEDGEMENTS

Thanks…

To Scot Danforth, for the original copywriting and publishing knowledge he shared as well as his valuable suggestions in organizing the materials.

To Elizabeth Genovise, for the line editing expertise she provided in correcting grammatical errors in the manuscript.

To Allan S. Philp, Ph.D. who led me through some of the darkest of times and helped me find my way into the light.

To friends who encouraged me to publish this book.

To my wife Peggy who cared for me when in the depths of depression, supported me when I was down, believed in me when I didn't believe in myself, whose faith was strong when mine was weak, and loved me through it all.

To the Good Lord who has given me life, blessed me beyond measure, and endowed me with a way with words.

TABLE OF CONTENTS

INTRODUCTION 7

CHAPTER 1 9

   ROADS OF TIME 9

      Who Was That Old Man?.. 11

      Time Has Made a Change in Me 12

      The Old Guitar 13

      The Christmas Tree 14

CHAPTER 2 15

   BACK ROADS 15

      You Can't Go Home 17

      Jackson's Crossing 18

      The Flour Mill 20

      "Uncle Doc" 21

      Preacher Man 23

      A Grandpa of My Own 24

      A Farmer's Conversation with God 25

      Forty-Acre Dreams 27

      They Dammed The "Little T" 28

      Piney Woods 29

CHAPTER 3 30

   ROAD OF NO RETURN 30

      What I'd Give Once More to Hear 32

      The End of the Road 33

      Cold, Cold Ground 34

      The Night The "Rat" Died 35

      100 Miles to Houston 36

      I Turned and You Were Gone 38

When Time is no More	39
What More Can I Say?	40
The Flickering Flame	41
I've Been There Too!	42

CHAPTER 4 43

The Lost Highway 43

Why?	45
What is The Point?	46
God, Why Did You Make Me?	47
Who Deals?	48
Inner Sanctum	50
The Great Deceiver	51
Lost Highway	52
Tell Me the Truth	54
A Prisoner of Time	56
Where Goes The Love of God?	57

CHAPTER 5 58

The Redemption Road 58

Somewhere Between	60
Eternal Life	61
Be Not Deceived!	63
The Light	64
Today I Met a Man	65
Who Am I?	66
Just Like Me?	67
I Think I'll Just Go Fishing!	68
The Old Dogwood Tree	69

CHAPTER 6 71

THE ROAD TO GOD 71

- Who Crucified Jesus? 73
- The Minstrel 74
- Nails of Love 76
- God's Gift to Man 78
- The Greatest Miracle 80
- Because of the Choice He Made 82
- Sing Me the Story 83
- When I Pray 84
- More than Just Words 85
- Judgment 86
- The Lion of Judah 88
- Imagine That! 89

CHAPTER 7 91

ROADS YET TRAVELED 91

- I Never Walk Alone 93
- Psalm 23 (Revised) 94
- To Sense God 96
- At Times 97
- Weep Not For Me 98
- About the Author 99
- Other work by G.W. Scott 100

INTRODUCTION

THIS IS A BOOK OF POETRY—poetry that tells stories about ordinary people, places, and things, and candidly probes for answers to the mysteries of life and ways of the world. Written in everyday language, a wide variety of subjects are addressed to which people from all walks of life can relate and enjoy reading.

However, the book is not just a random collection of poems—it serves a higher purpose. Read collectively, rhymes that will bring a smile to the face, a tear to the eye, a tug to the heart, and cause one to stop and ponder provide a synopsis of my life-long struggles to understand life, the world, and people. Integrated prose relates my reconciliation of those struggles against the backdrop of my Christian faith while battling depression. The book's ultimate purpose is to share the results of those struggles with others who have wrestled with faith, questioned life, or searched for peace.

Where Roads May Lead metaphorically portrays seven life events as traveling on different types of roads and exploring the destinations to which they may lead, e.g., "Road of No Return." I'm sure that you have traveled most, if not all, of these "roads" on your life journey also.

All roads lead somewhere, but where each may lead is not always predictable, and no two people have the same experience traveling the same road. Due to our unique experiences, we're led to different destinations and develop personal histories that define who and what we are. The physical, mental, emotional, and spiritual struggles that are an inherent part of this definitive process serve to mold and fashion our view of the world and perspective on life.

Of the poems in this book (which were written over several years), some were born out of the depths of depression; many were inspired by my "religious" experiences; several are an attempt to walk in other people's shoes; others are the product of an inquiring mind. Many of them came, I believe, as an inspiration from God. As a Christian, it is my conviction that every person has had unique life experiences, and that it is within our life's plan to share our stories with others.

Although most of these "roads" are normally traveled concurrently as a part of our life's journey, I've arranged them in a somewhat chronological order to indicate a logical progression through time. During this progress, with the help of doctors, counselors, pastors, and a loving wife, I've been able to develop distinct conclusions concerning these events, resolve personal issues related to the past, and reconcile struggles to understand contradictions between the world and spiritual faith.

I invite you to join me on a walk down these seven roads and share where traveling these roads has led me on my journey of discovery. Perhaps you may find somewhere within these pages some words of encouragement and understanding for "where *your* roads may lead." Godspeed!

G.W. Scott

CHAPTER 1
Roads of Time

WHEN I WAS A KID GROWING UP, it seemed that time moved along in slow motion. The long, lazy summers seemed to last a lifetime as they crept along at a snail's pace and it was like an eternity from one Christmas to the next. But as I've grown older, time has accelerated into warp drive. Now, we barely find time to work in a summer vacation and it seems we hardly get the Christmas decorations put away until it's time to get them out again.

It was recently brought to my attention that, for many years, I've been living on "roads of time," unaware of just how rapidly the years were slipping by and the changes that were taking place around me. I became acutely conscious of this fact on our grandson's birthday.

Our grandson just recently celebrated his thirteenth birthday. As my wife and I were discussing his up-coming birthday party and what we might give him for a gift, it suddenly dawned on us: "he's going to be a *teenager*!" We couldn't believe it! Our grandson was going to be a teenager. It seemed like it was only yesterday that he was born.

Good grief! It should be our *son* who was just turning thirteen. This eye-opener to the reality of our son's and grandson's ages set me to evaluate the road of time that I had been traveling. With a twinge of melancholy, the stark reality of the question struck me: "where did the years go?"

It's easy to see the changes occurring in the world in general, but not so easy to recognize (or admit) the changes that are taking place in one's self and personal world.

Traveling the "Roads of Time" has led me to an awakening experience of suddenly seeing the gray in my hair, the age in my eyes, the wrinkles in my face, and acknowledging the changes that time has made in me in order to consider my age and usefulness.

The roads of time may lead different people to different destinations on their journey through life. The poems in this chapter examine some changes effected by traveling this road.

Who Was That Old Man?

Today I met an old man; I looked closely at his face.
He seemed somewhat familiar, like I knew him from someplace.
A ghost from the days of youth? Could he be some old schoolmate?
There seemed a strange connection with this stranger at mind's gate.

A young chap well-acquainted only now in an aged form,
With countenance unmoving, a survivor of life's storm.
Surely this could not be he, this slight one of body frail,
Where once grew ebony mane now gray strands on shoulders fell.

The hollow eyes seemed distant, lost in some place dark and cold,
A face with deep carved features worth a hundred stories told.
I could not bear to face him; yet, I could not turn away,
To me, the man did not speak; to him, no words could I say.

At times we meet some person that we somehow seem to know,
At times we meet some person that we do not want to know.
But today in the mirror a stranger's face I did see,
I asked, "Who was that old man? No, surely not! Could it be?"

Time Has Made a Change in Me

Once I'd run and not tire 'cross fields and streams the day long,
Far into the midnight hour dance to the young reveler's song.
Now the steps are feebly slow, the back stooped and lowly bent,
No longer chase the heart's call; those days, they came and went.

It seems only yesterday, I was bright, virile and strong,
The future seemed so distant, lived for the day right or wrong.
The years sped by unnoticed while busy running life's race,
Time came and stole Adonis, left Methuselah in his place.

In the heyday of my youth, free to live as I pleased,
It was women, drink, and daring, life a trifle and a tease.
Now in hoary, moss-backed age, prisoner of decrepit bones,
No solace in such playthings, spirit cold as graveyard stones.

In days of wine and roses, we were married in our prime,
Placed rings of gold on fingers and pledged our love for all time.
Those days now but memories, Father Time did us betray,
Death as a thief at night came and took my loved one away.

The fickle sweet bird of youth took its flight and flew away,
I'd give my soul for that time if it be for just one day.
We of this moth-eaten race like the leaf that fades and falls,
Relics on human trash heaps, castaways inside home's walls.

The flower that blossomed in youth is now fading from life's stage,
Victim of fatal disease accursed, slow-consuming age.
The one who was within me will soon pass no more to be,
Can't long cheat the undertaker, Time has made a change in me.

The Old Guitar

The old guitar stands alone just inside the closet door,
Gathering the dust of time, no one plays it anymore.
Its finish scarred and faded, tattered strings now worn with age,
The toll of years on the road and one-night stands on the stage.

It was in the yesterdays nestled in the master's hands,
They would play the nights away making music for the fans.
Traveling life's road together, instrument and troubadour,
Corner bars to concert halls, neon lights to swinging doors.

Melodies flowed sweet and pure from the guitar's magic strings,
 Blending with the master's voice, homespun ballads that he'd sing.
Fingers gently strumming tunes, be they country, rock or blues,
Bringing forth cheers and applause and perhaps a tip or two.

Through ups and downs, good and bad, they had seen and done it all,
All are now just memories since that final curtain call.
Will some other master come, what will be the guitar's fate?
The old guitar stands alone, in the silent darkness waits.

The Christmas Tree

Not just anyone will do, that special tree must find,
Search through the evergreens for that one-of-a-kind.
In ornamented home the centerpiece to be,
Symbol of the season, the esteemed Christmas tree.

Then personally trimmed in shimmering attire,
In its own special place to treasure and admire.
Crowned with angel or star, twinkling lights all aglow,
Stands guard over treasures beneath branches below.

On floor barren of gifts the deserted tree stands,
Its booty all plundered by the family clan.
Folks no more gathered `round sharing holiday glee,
Red lights have ceased to shine on the green Christmas tree.

Christmas time is over, tree stripped of its dressing,
Now just another tree with no special blessing.
Having served its purpose, `tis a sad sight to see,
Lying there on the heap, the cast-off Christmas tree.

CHAPTER 2

Back Roads

THERE'S AN ANCIENT QUOTE THAT SAYS: "Yesterday is a memory, tomorrow is a mystery, today is a gift." While developing careers and raising families, we give more thought to the *todays* and *tomorrows*, living for today and planning for tomorrow. As we grow older, however, the *yesterdays* take on greater importance. In our later years, there seems to surface a natural tendency to recall the days of youth, an innate desire to connect with our roots, and a longing to go back "home."

I was raised in a farming community of rolling hills, pasture fields, and woodlands crisscrossed by the Tennessee River. It was a community of poor, hard-working farmers who lived a simple life, had a strong work ethic and kinship with the land, and a staunch religious faith. As a kid roaming those fields and woods, I developed a love of nature and a respect for the unpretentious way of life of the people there.

My family moved away from this rural setting while I was still a youngster. After growing up and graduating from college, I went on to a career that took me to large cities with their four-lane highways and Interstates—farther away from the dirt and gravel back roads of the country. But the sights and sounds of those early years never strayed far from my memory and I've often found myself time-traveling back in time down "back roads" of my mind to carefree summer days on the farm.

A few years ago, I went back for a visit, I found that to my dismay the farm now lies in a watery grave beneath a new lake—the people who lived there

15

had up-rooted and displaced. The high school I attended was gone, along with all the local haunts the kids used to gather at, and most of the people I knew had either moved away or died. A shopping mall was on the site where the drive-in movie theater had been and a new interstate highway now ran through the edge of town.

Traveling "back roads" has led me to the only place I can go "home" or recollect memories from the past. I remember things as they were then, but nothing stays the same as it was, for the passage of time takes its toll transforming the past into the present. "Yesterday is a memory" and the only place memories exist is somewhere on the back roads that wander along the hills and valleys of the mind.

Traveling these roads may lead to fond remembrances or to heart- breaking recollections. In the poems that follow, I document some of the characters, places, and experiences I recall traveling on back roads.

You Can't Go Home

Sometimes I go traveling down the back roads of time,
To a place we called home, Mom calling "Suppertime!"

School-free, barefoot summers, a tire swing in a pine,
Fishing with my friend Joe, swinging on monkey vines.

Biking on gravel roads, family cake walks at school,
Killing hogs, baling hay, and plowing with the mule.

Sunday school, revivals, and dinners on the ground,
Sitting on the front porch listening to the night sounds.

Went back for a visit, thought I'd look up old Joe,
A lake hides the home place, new faces I don't know.

Nothing is as it was; all the old haunts are gone,
Joe's dead ten years today, guess it's time to move on.

As for days of the past, they are forever gone,
We can but reminisce, for Time it marches on.

When you choose to wander, when you elect to roam,
And age has done its deed, you'll find you can't go home!

Jackson's Crossing

Just a wide spot in the road where dirt roads crossed the blacktop,
Ten miles from the nearest town, few travelers made this stop.
Just known as Jackson's Crossing to the folks who lived around,
Most of them simple farmers scratching a living from the ground.

On one side of the crossroads stood the Jackson grammar school,
Ms. Johnson was a teacher, tried to educate young fools.
Readin', writin', arithmetic, playing marbles on the ground,
When it came time for high school, the kids were bused to town.

Across the way from the school was the Brewsters' Grocery Store,
One gas pump and two screen doors with a coal stove on the floor.
Men gathered to play checkers, lunch on bologna and cheese,
Whittle sticks and swap stories over moon pies and RCs.

There was Mr. Sanders' place; his place was the Blacksmith shop,
Every day he'd fire his forge and stoke up the coals red hot.
He shaped horseshoes, shod horses and fashioned new wagon wheels,
He could hammer out any shape from the white-hot molten steel.

Just a piece back on Fork Creek was 'ole man Briton's floor mill,
He and two spinster sisters lived alone up on the hill.
People brought their wheat and corn to turn into flour and meal,
For fee or trade he would grind and shake on a business deal.

Down the road from the crossing was the Simpson's house and farm,
One sad day Mr. Simpson hanged himself there in the barn.
The Jackson's were our neighbors, had a son whose name was Bryan,
We played together often; he was a good friend of mine.

Then somewhere up the dirt road there'd come a sound all could tell,
The Riley boys on John Deere flying like two bats-out-of-Hell.
They'd streak across the blacktop changing those gears on the run,
Gravels flying, dust boiling, young hotrodders having fun.

Living there, I was a part of that wonderland each day,
Watched those people live their lives as they daily went their way.
Just hard-working humble folks who always took life in stride,
Those times of a simple life, seems they've gone away to hide.

The Flour Mill

The old flour mill stands dormant, a relic of the past,
A reminder of the days that time has caught and passed.
The waters no more flow through the old timeworn mill race,
Silent stands the wheels and stone that milled grain in this place.

The Miller's name was Oscar, Mister Briton to most,
With his sisters made a home, the old-maids formal hosts.
He was old and somewhat strange, a kind man tall and grey,
I can picture him today, a memory far away.

Farmers came from near and far with wheat and corn to deal,
Made a bargain with the man, then left with flour and meal.
For mom I'd buy Oscar's meal; he would in brown bag tie,
A peck to bake some cornbread, for two bits she would buy.

Those folks have long left the scene as has their life and times,
What tales the flour mill could tell, but in the tongue of mime.
The world it goes speeding by, most caring not a dime,
No more to be remembered but in some book or rhyme.

"Uncle Doc"

A hush fell over the house, the old man rose to his feet,
In a voice broken and slow, he sang with a spirit sweet.
Strains of "Wayfaring Stranger" caught hold the assembly's ears,
I call to mind the man well, though but a lad of ten years.

People called him "Uncle Doc," that's all I knew for a name,
Not how long he'd walked this earth nor from what place that he came.
He was that song that he sang; words in him bore flesh and bone,
Just looking for a better home than a house of clay, bed of stone.

In a deep, dark wrinkled face lay etched a novel in time,
And a pair of calloused hands forged in fields that took his prime.
With a longing in his voice, a hollowness in sad eyes,
For the loved ones laid to rest and a world that told him lies.

"Uncle Doc" was all alone except for a dog he called "Zeke,"
In a little one-room shack on the bank by Cedar Creek.
His wife had many years passed, children known only in dreams,
No kin to share his sorrow, only time on which to lean.

On the road that leads narrow, his chosen path for life's race,
Mountain tops and valleys low walked with a heart full of grace.
This least among God's children had his share of pain and woe,
Never turned away a soul who was lost and sinking low.

Loved by all those who knew him and all his quiet, strange ways,
I can hear that prayer meeting when some voice was heard to say,
"Sing the 'Wayfaring Stranger'" and 'ole "Doc" would smile and nod,
His eyes would tear to words of waking in the arms of God.

I've thought of his journey's end, other ways my pathway found, He long ago left this earth, loosed from its shackles that bound.
A pilgrim in a strange land, prisoner on an earthbound rock,
Wayfaring stranger no more, home at last is "Uncle Doc."

Preacher Man

He wore one old black suit and a faded red tie,
Now getting up in years, still young at heart and spry.
He traveled 'round about living out his life's plan,
To answer God's calling; he was a preacher man.

He'd slowly take in hand a Bible tattered old,
From its dog-eared pages preach the truths it did hold.
In his heated sermons warned of the Devil's spell,
Showed the way to Heaven and saved our souls from Hell.

A poor country preacher, a salary never knew,
Just a small collection from the folks in the pews.
He'd preach Sunday morning and then again that night,
And take Sunday dinner at some neighbor's invite.

Sometimes he'd come our way and spend the day with us,
Mom would get excited and always make a fuss.
She'd fill up the table—fried chicken, taters, peas,
We had to use manners, "Yes ma'am!" - "Thank you!" - "Please!"

He showed the love of God in kind and gentle ways,
His words hid in my heart still call from childhood days.
He'd kid us kids and say, "Guess a riddle if you can."
We didn't know his name; we just called him Preacher Man.

A Grandpa of My Own

Never had a live grandpa like many other kids,
To tell stories of the past and all the things he did.
Didn't get to meet the man, known only in my head,
For when I came on the scene he was already dead.

One time my Mama told me that grandpa's name was Jim,
That we were two-of-a-kind she said of me and him.
I imagine us today, the things we two could do,
Adventures shared together as only pals can do.

I talk to him now and then; he listens when I call,
From that old faded picture hanging there in the hall.
I tell him all my troubles; we share a laugh or two,
He's always there to listen and helps to see me through.

Never had a live grandpa but mine seems real to me,
I've felt his presence often somewhere inside of me.
He may be but a dream one, not one of flesh and bone,
But I have had a grandpa, a grandpa of my own.

A Farmer's Conversation with God

Howdy Lord, it's me again, here in the field today,
Got a few things on my mind, some things I wanna say.
Now, I know that yore busy savin' sinners from Hell,
But iffin ye got some time, I'd like to talk a spell.

I ain't askin' fergiveness fer all my many sins,
And I ain't come complainin' 'bout how bad things has been.
I ain't even gonna ask ye to do anything,
I jes wanna say Thank Ye! fer some blessins and things.

Little Jimmy broke his leg, it's healin' up real well,
And Ma's been feelin' poorly, she's had quite a sick spell.
But she's finally comin' 'round and feelin' right pert now,
And we've started gettin' milk from that 'ole dried up cow.

The beans ain't doin' too good because it's been real dry,
Looks like a good tater crop comin' in by and by.
Chickins is a-layin' good though the 'ole rooster died,
And I caught a mess of fish that we cleaned up and fried.

And, Lord, that big 'ole full moon you hung the other night,
There low over the cornfield shinin' yeller and bright.
With that gaggle of wild geese silhouetted in flight,
You know that really was an awful purty sight.

Got a letter from Henry, he's comin' home from the war,
Got all shot up and wounded, don't understand what for.
At least he's alive and well, he'll be here any day,
Take care of them other boys, keep 'um outta harm's way.

Lord, I hope you understand what I tryin' to say,
Fer words don't come as easy as does puttin' up hay.
You give me blessings in ways that I don't always see,
But when I open my eyes they're just all around me.

I'm much obliged to you God fer ye being so kind,
And all the things that you do fer this famly of mine.
Well, I thank you for listenin' and don't mean to complain,
But do you think you could send just a little more rain?

Forty-Acre Dreams

From a life on the farm I had longed to break free,
To escape country life and to the bright lights flee.
Fork Creek's forty acres for this boy held no ties,
I packed up what was mine and said all my goodbyes.

Spent the most of my life just traveling around,
Seen all this land's beauty, met people in her towns.
From bright lights of Broadway to a Vegas strip bet,
The top of 'Ole Smokey to a western sunset.

I have found some good times but no fortune or fame,
I have had some bad times learning to play The Game.
As more years pass me by, the older new things seem,
Thinking more on the past, having forty-acre dreams.

Distant voices beckon from somewhere deep inside,
Reminders of time lost and of loves that have died.
Wherever I may go, whatever I may seek,
The back roads of my mind carry me back to Fork Creek.

They Dammed The "Little T"

There's a big, winding river way down in Tennessee,
It has a smaller brother they call the "Little T."
For many generations it flowed through the countryside,
In nature's perfect setting with waters deep and wide.

Along this scenic river, many miles up and down,
There lived farming families coaxing life from the ground.
Their home for generations, raised kin, made their stand,
A clan of poor proud farmers poured their souls in the land.

But greedy politicians cast eyes upon this soil,
Plotted with developers to take it as their spoils.
"That bunch of 'ole dirt farmers don't need it anyway,
We can turn a big profit with playgrounds on a bay."

The farmers' land was taken, was taken for a song,
By greedy men with power, no sense of right or wrong.
So they dammed the "Little T" and created a new lake,
So they dammed the "Little T" for money they could make.

They wiped out that old river and aged farmland scenes,
Displaced all those families, stole their homes and their dreams.
Replaced them with country clubs, condos, yachts, and golf greens,
Cater to society's best, the moneyed kings and queens.

Now some will say that's progress, guess that's your point of view,
When people abuse their power but for the chosen few.
But that's the way it happens when they dam a "Little T,"
There's more losers than winners when they damn a "Little T."

Piney Woods

As a kid growing up in rural Piney Woods,
Life could be at times hard; folks did the best they could.
Just hard-working farmers living off red-clay land,
Neighbors aided neighbors when they needed a hand.

Meals were plain and simple, potatoes, bread, and beans;
Biscuits in the morning with cool milk from the spring.
The fare at times was small, just tea and cold cornbread,
No matter what the meal, a blessing still was said.

Each family lived the same, didn't know we were poor,
Naïve of things to want, then one can't wish for more.
I'd mount a horse of stick, strap on holstered cap gun,
And with a dog named Ponch, through Piney Woods we'd run.

We would search thru the pines, ramble over the hills,
Climb 'round the 'ole barn loft, race through the grassy fields.
Go wading in the creek, snatch crawdads from beneath rocks,
Do all the daily chores and care for the livestock.

Piney Woods are now gone, they lie beneath a lake,
Men dammed the "Little T" for money they could make.
Not by the farmers though, farms taken for a song,
By greedy men with power, no sense of right and wrong.

CHAPTER 3

Road of No Return

A FEW YEARS AGO, my wife's sister passed away at the age of forty-seven after losing her battle with cancer, which she had bravely resisted for several years. At the conclusion of the graveside service following her funeral, I remember walking away from the cemetery beside her elderly parents who had tried to care for their ailing daughter during her final months of suffering, and hearing one tearfully say to the other, "well, we've gone as far as we can go" and the other responding, "yes, we've come to the end of the road." Weary and discouraged, they had walked the "Road of No Return."

Of all the roads we have to travel in life, the road that leads through the valley of the shadow of death is the most difficult one to walk, and everyone must walk it sometime. It is a "road of no return" (at least as far as life on earth is concerned), for when a loved one is taken in death, they shall not return. We will never again on this earth see our departed one's smiling face walk through a door, share a meal with them, open Christmas presents with them, or feel their warm touch.

It can also be a "road of no return" for the ones left behind when it results in living a life filled with unresolved conflicts or regrets from which there is no absolution. I recall overhearing a young lady at her grandmother's funeral wishing she could bring her grandmother back to life for just a minute to tell her she loved her. She had showed her love to her in many ways but realized

that she had never actually spoken the words to her.
But the opportunity was gone forever!

Traveling the "Road of No Return" has led me to know that it is a road that leads to physical, mental, emotional, and spiritual testing, and reminds us of the uncertainty of life and the finality of death.

The road of no return may lead to sorrow and regret, but it can also lead to hope. The following poems relate stories of traveling this road.

What I'd Give Once More to Hear

I nourished him and dressed him, at night tucked him into bed,
We rough-housed and joked about and how many books were read.

Shooting hoops in the backyard and fly fishing, hooking trout,
Walking, talking through the woods, that we were pals was no doubt.

This my one and only son who made the days worth living,
Was the pleasure of my life and loved with all my being.

Through his schooling, sports, and church, grew up according to plan,
In body, in mind, in soul, developed into a man.

But then he was called away to that far-off Asian war,
Said he believed there were things you had to stand and fight for.

I shall not forget the day I waved to him from the docks,
I shall not forget the day I saw the flag-covered box.

A part of me died that day from a saddened, broken heart,
Didn't think I could go on with my world torn all apart.

A young life too soon ended only eighteen years from birth,
He's gone but not forgotten by those he touched here on earth.

I wonder how he'd look now, I reflect on what he'd be,
I hope that we'd still be pals; what happened to you and me?

Whenever I think of him and all the good times we had,
What I'd give once more to hear that little boy call me "Dad."

The End of the Road

Slowly she coaxed the needle into the vein in her arm,
"Just one more trip," she reasoned, "will not cause me any harm."
The venom through veins coursed cold 'til in brain was poison sewn,
Tripped out to where the last stop was at the end of the road.

Celebrating with good friends, year twenty-one on the town,
He reveled and he partied while pouring Jack Daniel's down.
With pedal to the metal one hundred ten the gauge showed,
When the 'vette left the highway and found the end of the road.

Sitting alone in a flat there on the city's south side,
Scribbled a note by streetlight stained by the tears that she cried.
Down to the Fifteenth Street Bridge she walked bearing pregnant load,
In the river's dark waters she reached the end of the road.

In a cheap downtown hotel they'd meet in secret affair,
A jealous spouse with a gun one grim night ended it there.
Two lovers sentenced to death, one to prison a life owed,
That night three people's lives crossed there at the end of the road.

Keeping up with the Joneses, in the material race,
Chasing America's Dream, living at a breakneck pace.
Then one day came the chest pain, the life blood no longer flowed,
Pronounced Dead On Arrival there at the end of the road.

In the way you live take care, and in the choices you make,
Things don't always go as planned; of this please make no mistake.
The foolish man dares tempt fate, per chance to leave earth's abode,
For there's a price to be paid there at the end of the road.

Cold, Cold Ground

It was a cold winter's day as best I now recall,
Snow dusted the frozen ground, the air filled with death's pall.
Out in the church's graveyard with mourners gathered 'round,
They laid sweet Polly Parson there in the cold, cold ground.

Time on earth was for her short, just twenty and one years,
Left a father's broken heart, a mother's thousand tears.
From the cradle to the grave by a parent's love bound,
They laid sweet Polly Parson there in the cold, cold ground.

She and I were pledged to wed with the coming of spring,
When winter's bleakness gives way to new life that it brings.
But an assailant within struck her frail body down,
They laid sweet Polly Parson there in the cold, cold ground.

So, farewell to the mountains and the fields where you've grown,
And farewell to the loved ones and the home that you've known.
Your race on earth now is run; your last sun has gone down,
They've laid sweet Polly Parson there in the cold, cold ground.

It was a strange twist of Fate took us both for a fall,
But greater than even life is love's beckoning call.
When I sleep in the evening, hear not the lone dove's sound,
Lay me with sweet Polly Parson there in the cold, cold ground.

The Night The "Rat" Died

I called him Mr. Davis but the men all called him "Rat,"
Always wore his overalls and an old worn-out straw hat.
Don't know how he got that name; I just never thought to ask,
Must be some good story there, some funny tale from the past.

My dad and "Rat" were farmers; they worked on the Bacon Farm,
Days lasted until sundown from the early morn's alarm.
They milked the cows, slopped the hogs and plowed dusty fields all day,
Picked tobacco, planted corn and then mowed and baled the hay.

I still remember it well; it was a Saturday night,
When the alarm for help came; the talk gave me quite a fright.
"Rat" was mowing after dark when he flipped his big John Deere,
Covered by hot leaking oil, trapped under the steering gear.

Men they came from all around, they labored all through the night,
Trying to free the trapped man, 'til the first morning's light.
Neighbors all pulled together and there were many prayers said,
But when the "Rat" was set free, Mr. Davis he was dead.

The sorrow touched not just one but families one and all.
Of this poor man's life and death, this one night's all I recall.
Killed by a big green tractor, the fact cannot be denied,
But that's the way it happened, there on the night the "Rat" died.

100 Miles to Houston

He wheeled his rig off the blacktop, stirring up gravels and dust,
At the Come-On-In Truck Stop as he silently cussed.
Time to stretch legs and unwind and then have him a cup,
Just a modern-day cowboy with horse trailer and truck.

He strolled in through the front door, softly walked 'cross the floor,
There was six-feet-two of him 'neath the Stetson he wore.
Got a window-side table, ordered breakfast for one,
His eyes spoke to the heartache of his father's only son.

Trying to sort through feelings, picked at bacon and eggs,
Too distracted to notice the waitress' shapely legs.
Riding the 'ole memory train back to times as a kid,
Of growing up on the ranch and things he and "Gramps" did.

He left a tip, paid the tab, stepped outside to a scene,
Two duds roughing up a man for the bills in his jeans.
A chill coursed through the cowboy, his blood pulsed fast and cold,
Something familiar touched him 'bout this man gray and old.

One went sprawling in the dirt from the blow his fist struck,
The other one, backing off, went running for his truck.
Cowboy picked the old man up, helped him in the Come-On-In,
To salute the old man's thanks tipped his hat'n flashed a grin.

He checked all the trailer tires, stroked "Rusty" thru the gate,
That pony was a champion, best in the Lone Star State.
Climbing back into the cab, eyed the picture awhile,
Hanging there on the dashboard, "Gramps" with his country smile.

It had just been him and "Gramps" since he was only eight,
On forty Houston acres they called The "Lazy H."
He'd started ridin' rodeo to try and make ends meet,
Had been out on the road now for just about two weeks.

He had stopped over in Fort Worth to ride in one more show,
Getting ready to head home when they came to let'em know.
A rancher neighbor found him, said he passed in the night,
Packed up his gear, hit the road, cowboy drove in the quiet.

The closer to home he got, he just wanted to run, Just saddle up 'ole "Rusty," ride off into the sun.
Things would never be the same with "Gramps" laid in the ground,
The green interstate sign said, 100 miles to Houston town.

I Turned and You Were Gone

When you were just a babe I'd sit you on my arm,
Not as often as I should with your disarming charm.
Busy with my own plans as how life would be styled,
I turned and you were gone, my babe was now a child.

You did the normal things, Little League and Boy Scouts,
It was mom always there excusing my copouts.
Busy making money, was seldom at home seen,
I turned and you were gone, my child was now a teen.

You were quite the athlete, the high school sports all-star,
Saw you play once or twice but bought you that new car!
Climbing up the ladder, gave all it did demand,
I turned and you were gone, my teen was now a man.

Reached the top and retired, met the goals on life's list,
Now I have time to do all the things that we missed.
I promised you back then and I do what I say,
I'd make it up to you somewhere along the way.

Sorry Dad, I can't now, have my own family,
With a new job and all and responsibility.
Going with some buddies to hike and mountain climb,
With kids' games and school plays, maybe some other time.

I turned and you were gone, another verse, same song,
Too late to make amends, to make rights out of wrongs.
I let you slip away marching in life's parade,
I turned and you were gone, a child lost the price paid.

When Time is no More

Created from dust, man returns to dust,
For wages of sin, the Judge will be just.
The poor man but seeks the daily bread's crust,
The rich man to fill his selfish heart's lust.

In Adam's treasures, put not your heart's trust,
For treasures of earth, they mold and they rust.
As darkness of night is chased by the sun,
When time is no more, mankind's race is run.

Seasons have their rank, a time for all things,
To draw the saber and make a verse ring.
Offer up the cheek; take eye-for-an-eye,
Draw lines in the sand, learn to question why.

The frail rose must dwell among briars and thorns,
Where virtue is stained, innocence doth mourn.
Reckoning will come when sin tenders its wage,
And the vine is pruned for the coming age.

What More Can I Say?

From dust to dust they come and they go,
The pages are turned and the book is closed.
When twelve chimes the clock for the close of day,
Known but in picture and a child at play.

From ashes to ashes they rise and they fall,
On history's stage, play out destiny's call.
Swept from the earth's face by the winds of time,
Left but in mem'ries and words of a rhyme.

From Alpha to Omega, from beginning to end,
A story is told in a Book, then penned,
Of how it would be of women and men,
Of good and evil, of love and of sin.

For all a season, to rejoice and mourn,
A loss and a gain and a soul reborn.
When time has yielded, dust and ash give way,
To all that is new; what more can I say?

The Flickering Flame

The flickering candle flame so silently does glow,
In its picturesque display does the candle's life show.
Life born from the glowing fire upon the candlestick,
Does venerate its maker throughout the burning wick.

The candle's glow lights the night to make the darkness flee,
With a soft and gentle warmth to help the footstep see.
A beacon in the window, a guide home to the lost,
A quiet comfort for the soul drawn to it like the moth.

The candle's flame burns strongly, licking, leaping with flare,
Illuminating the room perched on the mantle there.
Yet, the candle's life is frail, but a flicker away,
From vanishing from the scene in a stream of smoke gray.

A breath of air strokes the flame, the candle's left unburned,
Balanced between flame and smoke, life's lesson again learned.
An eternal flame does burn there in the Great Unknown,
A flickering flame it's not, for it burns on and on.

I've Been There Too!

Is the hurting too much in a body of pain?
You can no more endure all the physical strain?
I know of your anguish. I share the hurt with you.
Crucified on a cross, you know I've been there too!

Are you tired and weary, the world beaten you down,
Clouds of despair gather, only worries to be found?
Feeling lost and alone when few friends remain true,
Once on Calvary's hill, you know I've been there too!

Has your heart been broken by some word or some act,
By a special someone who has now turned their back?
I know the place you are in for this heartache I knew,
All alone on a cross, you know I've been there too!

Have you by a bedside held fast some dying hand,
Walked in some dark valley or in Death's shadow stand?
This path I have traveled as each person must do,
For three days in a tomb, you know I've been there too!

Do you dream of Heaven, a home beyond the grave?
Wonder if there's a place where streets with gold are paved?
Upon my Father's Word, I surely tell you true,
That Heaven's really real; you know I've been there too!

CHAPTER 4

The Lost Highway

EARLY IN THE MORNING on April 16, 2007, a student armed with .22 caliber and 9 mm handguns entered a resident hall on the campus of Virginia Tech University in Blacksburg, Virginia, and murdered two students. Approximately two hours later, the gunman entered a campus classroom facility, chained and locked the doors, and launched a random shooting spree. Marching up and down the halls, returning to some classrooms multiple times, the shooter relentlessly rained a hail of bullets on the defenseless occupants before turning his weapons upon himself. With the guns silenced, the bodies of five faculty members and twenty-five additional students lay silent in death. Twenty-five more lay wounded—all victims of a senseless massacre.

Incidences such as this have become commonplace in our world, and they cause us to question *why*? Not just why do the incidents happen, but why do certain individuals become the victims while others do not. Why is the passenger in a car crash killed and the driver not? Why is a child stricken with a disease and a serial killer not? Why does a tornado destroy one house and not the one next door?

For ages, philosophers, scholars, poets, and theologians have contemplated and debated the *whys* of life with no definitive conclusions drawn. Throughout history, people have continually struggled to make sense of the unexplainable injustices and tragedies that occur in this asylum we call the world, where the inmates are running amuck, creating chaos on every hand, and no one seems to be in charge. It's as if we're speeding down "the lost highway" and it has no exits. Even the Psalmist questioned, "Why are the nations in turmoil? Why do the peoples hatch their futile plots?" (Psalms 2:1-2 NEB)

Traveling "The Lost Highway" has led me to believe that there is no logic in the way the world operates and no rhyme or reason to the way life plays out in the course of people's lives, at least as far as mankind is concerned. In his song "Are The Good Times Really Over For Good" country music singer Merle Haggard asks if the country is going to hell and losing its culture of patriotism and liberty.

I doubt that anyone can answer that question with any degree of certainty. Neither the world nor life can be understandable to man, because it is not within the capacity of the finite human mind and spirit to comprehend the infinite complexities of all creation.

All roads lead somewhere, but where "The Lost Highway" may lead, God only knows! In this chapter, the poems probe for answers to questions traveling the lost highway.

Why?

Why is life so vexing, an endless uphill climb?
Be it Heaven's judgment for unnamed sin or crime?
Daily toils and struggles, to these are there no end?
With each day dawns new woe and to the weight I bend.

Must I my brother keep and bear my neighbor's load?
Sacrifice the harvest of seeds that I have sowed?
I cry out to my God as Job of olden years,
But yet to no avail; my ear no answer hears.

The body it grows weak, the mind is all in spin,
The soul cries for release from dreams of where I've been.
Oh! For but chance to run, to some distant place flee,
Escape life's sentence bound 'til by death am set free.

Try to live by The Book and to follow man's laws,
Yet how doth it profit but some luck of the draw?
Rain falls on one and all, life's not fair that's no lie,
But for the just man so, I can but question . . . Why?

What is The Point?
(based on the book of Ecclesiastes)

A man sows a garden with plants of many kinds,
Tends it year after year, in death leaves it behind.
Soon proof of his being and labor no more found,
By the winds of time swept into dust of the ground.

To pursue a life's dream is like chasing the wind,
It leads hither and yon and blows out in the end.
So live for the moment; now eat, drink, and be gay,
This too is emptiness; pleasure lasts but a day.

We seek titles and crowns, build monuments and towers,
Store up nest eggs of gold and lay claim to what's ours.
But this too is folly; earth's treasures fade away,
Forgotten by history, the victims of decay.

To a life man is born but to die at some age,
His time but a moment to appear on life's stage.
Why this way come and go, to vain labor appoint?
In the end all is lost, so just what is the point?

God, Why Did You Make Me?

Peering into the river's deep, dark waters below,
For chance to drown my sorrows there in its murky flow.
For I'm but an empty shell, a soulless body be;
I beg a question's answer: "God, why did you make me?"

Deserted by a father with no need for a kid,
A nameless, faceless someone, just a drunk on the skids.
Abandoned by a mother, left at a stranger's door,
To be a mom not her style, one of Sugar Man's whores.

Grew up hard in the state home, learned to be lean and mean,
Couldn't stay there forever, turned away when eighteen.
Tried to make it in the streets, no life there could I see,
I still seek for an answer: "God, why did you make me?"

Wandering aimless like a stray, nowhere to find a job,
With no means to make my way, a liquor store did rob.
When prison time has been served, not much for an ex-con,
The shelter's free cup of soup and a pint of blood pawn.

In the mire of life's quicksand, I'm sinking further down,
With no way up, no way out, would one care if I drowned?
For what sin am I punished? Why must life so cruel be?
I'm still wait for an answer: "God, why did you make me?"

If I but step from this ledge, sink into the abyss,
What awaits beyond the gloom, at worst no worse than this.
If not conceived in the womb, better would have been for me,
Where may I the answer find: "God, why did you make me?"

Who Deals?

Sitting on a bed staring at black brew in a cup,
In a backstreet mission shelter where the hopeless wind up.
Nothing but holes in my pockets, my whole world in a sack,
Wondering how I got here, can I find my way back?

Now there's some people tell me all you need do is pray,
If you'll just trust and have faith there'll be a brighter day.
But it was Life dealt the cards, it seems the deck was stacked;
The Joker's hand won the draw so my dreams were hi-jacked.

Even though you labor hard and by justice you live,
Life is the big man's to take, the little man's to give.
"Where there's a will, there's a way," or that's what I've been told,
But the will soon grows weary when no way does unfold.

Has there been laid master plans for each life that's unknown?
A prepared pathway through life for each person his own?
Why then are some people's roads laid out smooth, flat and straight?
While the roadways of others have hills, valleys and gates?

Are we humans but mere pawns on an earthen chess board,
For amusement at the whims of spiritual lords?
If God on High's in control, why's the world such a mess?
Trusting man here on his own? Perhaps it is a test!

When good fortune comes our way we claim right place, right time!
When misfortune makes a call we cry wrong place, wrong time!
Every person has a choice if covered by free will;
So choose carefully what you may, be it to heal or kill.

Make your way to confession; place some coins in the plate,
Read the horoscope's warning and hope it's not too late.
Seek some change for tomorrow while praying on the pew;
Pink slip comes in the morning for nothing's ever new.

Getting along in this world is hard and demanding.
Just making sense of it all is beyond understanding.
Time spent upon the shrink's couch being psychoanalyzed,
Finding that life holds no truth is life's truth realized.

Is it free will, chance, or fate? Or is God in command?
When does Lady Luck step in? Does Satan play a hand?
Is there one dealer alone who deals all the cards shown?
Do all come to the table to add cards of their own?

Inner Sanctum

I unlocked and opened my door in response to a knock heard there,
A stranger bid me to follow up the descending spiral stairs.
The farther down I did ascend, the higher up the staircase dropped,
And when I reached the final step the bottom was the very top.

My guide led me into a room, its walls mirrored and round within,
Could not escape my reflection, no place to run I hadn't been.
Moving farther from the mirror, a clearer image of it got,
Of mortals, demons, and angels, and a mad mind's sinister plot.

Then led into a judgment hall, windowless walls stark-white and square,
Tragic figures sat 'round a desk, a white-haired judge upon a chair.
Is innocence of guilt resolved? Guilt of innocence decided?
Is the answer in punishment or in how the mind's eye's guided?

My guide opened one last door; it led into the bright sunshine,
Winds of freedom blew through the trees and opened the eyes of the blind.
Who can say who's sane and who's not; does one end where the next begins?
Is man appointed to decide, just what is and is not sin?

The Great Deceiver

Life with your mask and charade, great deceiver of men,
Does your true nature conceal, pretending to be a friend?
My dreams for you have vanished, your promises now lies,
Broke the heart of my dearest who waits alone and cries.

I've toiled year in and year out as your slave in the field,
Yet in the end nothing gained from the crops' meager yield.
You tempt with visions of gold, but in your betrayal, Sentenced to life's
Lost and Found around breadless table.

Your yoke is harsh and heavy, your load I cannot bear,
Weary of body and spirit, to your chosen fate I'm heir.
You feed the fat, thrive the corrupt, prosper the rich man's son,
Deny the lean, fail the honest, enslave the poor man's son.

"What is life?" man petitions, although rhetorically;
He finds in the mocking silence no answer to his plea.
Don't worry, troublesome Life, you'll not yet have your way,
On pale horse there comes a riding friend Death to save the day.

Lost Highway

Is there yet time to believe, submit the price one must pay?
Or have I traveled too long down on old Hank's Lost Highway?[1]
When life's journey has ended, does the road traveled extend?
Or but a sign there posted, sadly declaring "Dead End?"

The man on the radio has all the answers, I'm told,
If I'll just send him five bucks they say he'll sure save my soul.
They sell Ole Time Religion at the new church down the street,
If I'll be a believer one day The Savior I'll meet.

On the right way to do it there's very few can agree,
Every group thinks that they're right, that's rather easy to see.
You have to go to my church, you have to worship my way,
Walk the same way that I walk and say the same things I say.

The Baptists say immersion, the Methodists say sprinkle,
Apostolics say ain't so, we've got another wrinkle.
'Rollers say get The Spirit, Scientists say Faith for the pained,
Presbyterians tell you, you know it's all pre-ordained.

Hindus believe you get there through much reincarnation,
It's the Five Pillars of Faith for the Islamic Nation.
Buddhism claims the truth of following the Eightfold Path,
Christianity the Cross the means to avoid God's wrath.

The atheist staunchly claims religion's all a great hoax,
 Either way say agnostics, "there's no way to prove it folks!"
Many teachers and thinkers, philosophers and poets,
Say we're all part of one whole, just look within to know it.

Catholics are absolved of sin and take the sacrament too,
Seek the coming Messiah the proclamation of Jews.
It is the way of Mormon for the followers of Young,
For others meditation is the message that is sung.

Some like contemporary some prefer traditional,
But if you worship with us it must be conditional.
Don't wear those stuffy choir robes, keep those guitars out of sight,
You should know it's plain to see that God knows that our way's right.

You're not like our people here; you just don't seem to fit in,
And the way that you appear is surely some sort of sin.
Your clothes are much too shabby and the hair's simply too long,
From the lower side of town and of course your color's wrong.

There's theologians and popes along with priests and preachers,
All selling their religion, touting all of its features,
So then whose claim is a lie and whose declaration truth?
Who does truly know the way and wherein does lie the proof?

Belief systems and dogmas, they form an unending list,
I've examined all of them, or is there one that I've missed?
Is redemption out of reach, the hour is late left to pray,
For I've about reached the end of 'ole Hank's Lost Highway[1].

As I ponder on it all inside a drug-induced haze,
While through the empty bottom of a glass bottle
I gaze Where in this holy riddle is found the Divine Figure?
Can you my questions answer before I squeeze this trigger?

[1] In 1950, Country Music artist Hank Williams, Sr. recorded the song "The Lost Highway," composed by Leon Payne in 1949, in which a man questions if he has passed the point of redemption due to the life he has led.

Tell Me the Truth

Archives overflow with books penned through history by man,
In his search to find the truth, his desire to understand.
There recorded all he knows, everything that he has learned,
The great things he's seen and done, and for answers he has yearned.

This pursuit has ferried him on a never ending quest,
Explored the world far and wide, north to south and east to west.
Built great cities and machines and all the sciences studied,
Earth and universe explored, many battlefields bloodied.

Just when is the truth the truth and when is the truth a lie?
Go and ask the atheist; to the both he will deny.
Just when is a lie a lie and when is a lie the truth?
Go and ask the lawyer man, for either he needs no proof.

Now do you say what you mean or do you mean what you say?
One may truly be the wish, but it's not always that way.
Now do you mean what you say or do you say what you mean?
One may intend tell no lie but may sound not what they seem.

Do you promise to speak truth and to God do you this swear?
"Yes" unless to do not so, one could avoid prison's snare.
"Until death do we two part" do you promise to be true?
"Yes," unless to do not so, one could win some love anew.

We are told on every hand, follow society's gaze,
Truth is as the eye beholds, one can see it many ways.
They say the old ways are bad; they're intolerant and wrong,
Truth and freedom have no bounds; it's time to sing a new song.

54

I looked within for some truth, talked with me and then all three,
I asked Body, Mind, and Soul, they that make up all of me.
Body said, "On this life's path, truth I tell you if I must,
There's been an old man following and he's catching up to us."

Mind said, "Yes, I'll tell you truth, it is somewhere in my head,
Don't remember like days past, now what was it that you said?"
Soul said, "Truth's not a mystery, it cannot be bought or sold,
You just go and read The Book, believe in The Story told."

Oh! Who am I to question wisdom of the world's great minds?
Just seems to me this old world is full of blind leading blind.
Just waxing philosophic, anyway, can't cause no harm,
But now it's time for supper here at the Shady Rest Farm!

A Prisoner of Time

You can have your suits and ties and the starched white collars,
Wall Street offices and phones and pursuit of dollars.
Give me a Stetson and jeans, a pair of spurs and boots,
An 'ole ranch house on the range, just get back to my roots.

The city's just too crowded, high-rises fence me in,
And dirty sidewalks take me where I've already been.
Where the buffalo once roamed, my spirit's there set free,
To ride along with the wind, just my pony and me.

On a summer's moonlit night, some old friends come along,
We sleep out under the stars and join in campfire songs.
We reminisce on the past about when the west was young,
Before all the rails were laid and all the wire was strung.

Days when a man traveled light with just a gun and saddle,
Time when he was his own boss and he fought his own battles.
But time has changed everything, even the cowboy's way,
Now I drive a BMW; that's moving up they say.

But no matter what the ride it's still the great outdoors,
It sure beats suffocating on the twenty-fifth floor.
I've got to call the limo; boss is at the airport,
Running late for a meeting, he'll be wanting that report.

Where Goes The Love of God?

Where goes the love of God when men die on the field,
The helpless are displaced and innocent are killed?
Where poverty is found in a mom's saddened eyes,
In a dad's broken heart and a child's hungry cries?

Where goes the love of God when family's blood is shed,
Men covet all they see and lie in sinner's bed?
The drug lord peddles death, the mad one random kills,
The terrorist sells fear, the politician deals?

Where goes the love of God when some there on the pews,
Whose lives are but a lie subvert the righteous few?
The womb's denied its life, playing by different rules,
Nature is perverted; going armed in the schools?

Where goes the love of God? It's always at the door!
But cold and hardened hearts can hear its knock no more.
Man's will to seek his own, desire to rule and rod,
Have filled up all the room, where goes the love of God.

CHAPTER 5

The Redemption Road

THE YOUNG BOY TIGHTLY CLUTCHED the knob of the kitchen door, holding it slightly ajar, as he stood trembling in the grip of fear with tears streaming down his face. A few feet away his parents were engaged in yet another yelling, name-calling, knock-down-drag-out fight in their on-going personal war. The boy's pleas for a truce were always met with rebuffs to "shut up." He clung to that door, ready to throw it open in an instant if things turned bad (as he believed they might) and run. Run to where he didn't know, but he knew he had to be in a place where he would be able to get out of that house quickly and get away.

That boy was me. My home life was dominated by bitter hostilities between my parents, interspersed with periods of unbearable tension. There were times when the arguments and fights escalated to a point that I literally feared for my life. The remainder of the time the atmosphere was one of nerve-racking anxiety. I hated home. It was the worst place I could be and I used any excuse to stay away as long as I could.

All my adult life, I've been haunted by recurring nightmares of those times, and have had an ongoing battle with depression due to the anger and resentment I've harbored toward my parents and the home environment created by their personal wars.

However, in recent years I began traveling "the redemption road," seeking to exorcise the "demons" from the past that have plagued me for so long. Through the guidance of an excellent therapist, I learned one particular lesson that is well illustrated by the following scene from the movie "Indiana Jones and The Last Crusade."

Indiana Jones and his father are battling the German Nazis for possession of the Holy Grail which has been discovered. During the course of the skirmish, an earthquake rips open the ground and the Holy Grail falls into a crevice, coming to rest on a ledge. With his father holding his legs, "Indy" stretches downward, reaching in a vain attempt to retrieve the cup lying just agonizing inches beyond his finger's reach in deference to the pleas of his father to just let it go.

Traveling "The Redemption Road" led me to a place where I was able to find deliverance from the disturbing nightmares and pressure-cooker anger. There are things that happen to us that, for whatever reason, can't be undone or forgotten. Memories can't be erased; scars will always remain. So, we must find some place between the memories and where we are now where we can come to terms with the hurt, learn to forgive and be forgiven, and "let it go."

The redemption road may lead to deliverance only for those who seek it. The poems in this chapter set forth examples of seeking deliverance.

Somewhere Between

I was somewhere between a boy and a man,
I was smarter than most, I had my own plan.
But a wasted life lived chasing faded dreams,
Got lost in illusions somewhere between.

It was somewhere between what's right and what's wrong,
A decision was made to follow along.
Spent a life behind bars, caught at the crime scene,
A wrong turn was taken somewhere between.

It was somewhere between stained glass and neon signs,
Traded altars and juice for bar stools and wine.
Mogen David and I on each other now lean,
 Sold out to the Devil somewhere between.

It was somewhere between Heaven and Hell,
In a war waged for souls there's a tale they tell,
Of a sacrifice made for souls to redeem,
Born again at a cross somewhere between.

It is somewhere between there and where you are.
Does where you want to be seem so very far?
Cease not your searching for the hand unseen;
The answer's to be found somewhere between.

Eternal Life

From Adam's great fall to man came a great curse,
For life as a mortal was to man nothing worse.
Thus man's undying thirst throughout all history,
Fuels his unending quest for immortality.

Resolute in his search for a fountain of youth,
But to its existence he has yet to find proof.
Eternally to live and not ever grow old,
To cheat Death its promise is his ultimate goal.

What if potion be found to allow man to wait,
'Til heart's wants be sated in present human state?
Preserve beauty and youth, be not old age's slave,
To live as immortal, lay not claim to the grave.

What price would men tender for a share of the brew?
Available to all or but a privileged few?
Just how far might he go to possess such a prize?
Cheat, steal, bribe and deceive, perhaps kill and tell lies?

On what would you wager? Just what fee would you pay?
To shun the Grim Reaper when time forfeits the day?
For a life eternal in blissful realms abide,
Feast at royal banquet as honored groom and bride.

Be assured now, my friend, a fount truly exists,
With living water flows; 'tis not fiction or myth.
Mystery to the blind, its truth comes to the light,
Be a curse to the wrong but blessing to the right.

But take heed where you search, be not deceived by lies;
That leads to the darkness, the cost wailing and cries.
From the chalice of Truth let thy lips only drink,
Therein lays the treasure, the price less than you think.

Be Not Deceived!

Hideous dark clouds shroud the sun and despondent sky does gloom,
A sickly pall falls o'er the land and casts evil spell of doom.
What doth disturb Plato's slumber within caverns hidden deep?
Apostates dare the pure to tempt and make poor lost souls to weep?

Beware my soul the Wicked One, wiles intoxicating sweet,
Let not beguiling trick deceive; bow down not before his feet.
My God, my God, I am but dead, my soul cries out from Sheol,
Grant me delay from sin's payday, mercy for a wandering soul.

My blood runs cold at ghastly sights, notions of fear clutch my chest,
The beast draws nigh with cruel delight; I shrink from the profane guest.
I beseech thee demon to flee and pray not my spirit breech!
Be gone to thy master's abode far from my soul to be reached.

Entrapped in a cosmic vortex, gnashing teeth and devilish screams,
War doth rage with red-eyed dragon and lion with eagle's wings.
Played out in unseen dimension, truth infused in my essence,
Free me from earthbound conditions, linger me in omniscience.

But spare me thy welcome Hades, so thy ease Purgatory,
I long for Elysium's fields or other such place of glory.
I survey from time's mountaintop eternity's land received,
With foe cast down from Heaven's reign; from the Truth be not deceived!

The Light

Darting about through Chaos like some battered wind-blown kite,
On a dark lonely voyage harbored in the Land of Bright.
I inquired of a stranger, "Is this the way I should go?"
"Believe me," said the Dark Man, "when I say both 'Yes' and 'No.'"

The sun fades into darkness yet the light grows in the land,
This traveler seeks an answer to the secret in his hand.
My head spirals and unfolds as with knife an apple peeled,
The mind blowing in the wind, a soul longing to be filled.

I stand on the precipice, peer long into the abyss,
Drawn to leap into the pit, damned by Insanity's kiss.
In Panic's arms I stand embraced; I tremble weakly with fear,
But where to run, where to hide, there's no place far, no place near!

I search madly to my left trying to locate the right,
But meet myself coming back going to the very same site.
Journey to a higher plane takes the pathway of the meek,
Will footsteps of the Righteous lead me to the place I seek?

Do I dare walk with angels? Be I mad or be I sane?
Is it real or just a dream, can anyone here explain?
Yet doth wisp of candle flame burst into burning life bright,
To reveal the mystery that leads onward to The Light.

Today I Met a Man

Today I met a man up there in Blackstone Jail,
Guilty of some vile deed, no one could pay his bail.
His sweat and tears now fall upon the 'ole rock pile,
The price the debtor pays who walks a crooked mile.

Today I met a man while riding on the rails,
His eyes looked like the sound of the train whistle's wail.
A boxcar to call home, a life without its strings,
Just following the tracks like a bird on its wings.

Today I met a man in a chauffeured limousine,
A claim to fame was his, toast of the social scene.
Barred from the world to live in isolation's pall,
Locked behind gates of iron in empty mansion halls.

Today I met a man, such a good man he was,
He preached a better way and stood firm for his cause.
Although mobbed and beaten until his life was through,
He freely gave his life, the cost for all sin's dues.

Who Am I?

We meet most everyday somewhere there in the streets,
You look the other way for chance our eyes should meet.
Really not so different, but not equal that's a fact,
You walk a higher road than my side of the tracks.
Who am I?

I see your scornful stares; hear whispers as you pass,
For the child that I bear I'm seen as lower class.
For this young girl's sin, yours may not be the same,
For a right to throw stones you surely can't lay claim.
Who am I?

Visiting at your church, there were no open arms,
Though your sign said "Welcome," my presence caused alarm.
My clothing raised eyebrows, my hair was judged too long,
Your lips sang hymns of love, but heart's a different song.
Who am I?

Many types of people created in the land,
Though God uniquely formed, some bear the world's brand. Some feel they are better, set apart from others,
They're birds-of-a-feather; some can't be their brothers.
Who am I?

Who am I but a sinner struggling with wrong and right?
Who am I but a stranger wandering lost in the night?
Who am I but a child of the least, last, and lost?
Who am I but a man crucified on a cross?
Who am I?

Just Like Me?

Visiting a small town, to an old church I went,
A sign there on a wall, a question did present.
"If every member of this church were just like me,
What kind of church would this church be?"

The words they struck a chord somewhere deep within,
My mind set to thinking as I read them o'er again.
As to the verse's meaning, of a truth there to see,
I pondered its challenge and the answer asked of me.

When the doors are open, if all attend as I do,
Would all the pews be full or just a paltry few?
If each gave gifts as I when passed the offering plate,
Could we meet the budget or would the bills be late?

Who would be in service if following my lead?
Would there be ministries for worship and to feed?
Would God's work get done or much just be ignored?
Could the church even be; would we just close the doors?

Answering to the verse drew pictures in my mind,
Of a church whose members are made up of my kind.
A sobering truth revealed, in a simple rhyme see,
When one's eyes are opened to its theology.

Stop for just a moment, read the verses anew,
Ponder again on the words; what do they say to you?
"If every member of *my* church were just like *me*,
What kind of church would *my* church be?"

I Think I'll Just Go Fishing!

You know life just really stinks; this world's quite a sorry place,
I've 'bout had it up to here with the wretched human race.
Nothing ever goes my way, just can't seem to get a break,
Always taking two steps back for each step ahead I take.

My 401's gone way down, heavy on my mind it weighs,
Been two years now at the plant since they've given me a raise.
My neighbor sued me in court, some drunk driver hit my truck,
They took my pension plan away, ain't had nothing but bad luck.

I saw a man with no legs, a homeless one on the street,
Lines of people hunting jobs, kids without shoes on their feet.
I ran into my friend Tom, the docs say he won't live long,
Victims of disease and crime with all their hopes and dreams gone.

A friend's house burned yesterday, another's kid's hooked on crack,
They were saying down at work someone's son died in Iraq.
My Uncle Jack passed away, was shot and killed for a buck,
TV cameras broadcast war, newspapers all filled with muck.

I guess my life's pretty good; my world's really not so bad,
We're all home doing well, and for that I'm really glad.
Have all we need and work's steady, no reason to be wishing,
It's such a good day today; I think I'll just go fishing!

The Old Dogwood Tree

Within view of my window there stands an old dogwood tree,
Reflecting on its features, it reminds me much of me.
Standing there in solitude looking lonesome and alone,
Its limbs gnarled and twisted marking the years it has known.

It shields lilies from the heat with a covering of shade,
Among its swaying branches a bird's nest is safely made.
With snow-white blooms in the spring and leaves of blood in the fall,
Reflect my life's road traveled before and after Cain's call.

An evil mind with a knife took my wife and baby's life,
With a shotgun I took his and a heart with hatred rife.
For many years I did run but the ghosts could not escape,
Demons and angels for my soul vie at Heaven's and Hell's gates.

I gave myself to the Sheriff; he locked me up in his jail,
Everything I had was lost, not one soul to go my bail.
The old judge showed no mercy, said, "I sentence you to hang,
At noon a week from Monday though I would have done the same."

Each day I eye the dogwood from the window of my cell,
It's as if it tries to speak but is concealed beneath a veil.
As though it's beckoning me to a place of rest and peace,
To lay me down in its shade would be such a sweet release.

The Man came in at noonday; he said, "it's now time to go,"
A padre walks beside me; my steps are thoughtful and slow.
I see clear the dogwood tree as I mount the wood platform,
Is time spent for wretch as me to hope for a soul reborn?

Warden, you asked of me this day to grant one last request,
There's just one thing you can do when my body's laid to rest.
When this work's done on your gallows and you've set my spirit free,
Would you bury me in the shade under the old dogwood tree?

CHAPTER 6

The Road to God

I WAS RAISED IN CHURCH and became a Christian as a teenager. But for most of my life, the church had been a place of condemnation and hypocrisy; religion, adherence to a set of "thou shalt not's" enforced by fear and guilt; and God, a fearful enforcer of rules waiting to strike down anyone who strayed from the straight-and-narrow. I became skeptical of the "religion" I saw demonstrated inside the walls of the church when contrasted with the behavior exhibited in the lives of church members both inside and outside the church.

My religious experiences had not measured up to my understanding of what Christianity is all about, and so I had become disillusioned with "church." However, my continuing spiritual journey has been one of discovery while traveling "the road to God"—a discovery of what the true church is and is not.

Over two-thousand years ago, people nailed Jesus Christ to a wooden cross with iron spikes and sentenced him to a tormenting death by crucifixion. Why? Because they feared him and the changes his "new Way" of serving God and relating to people would bring to the old order.

All these years later, things haven't changed. People still crucify him every day, not on a wooden cross with nails of iron, but on a spiritual cross with nails of self-righteousness, bigotry, and hypocrisy. Why? Because they fear him and the demanding standards of his "way" of serving God and relating to people have on their desire for a god and religion that can be twisted and shaped to accommodate their own personal likes and dislikes.

Traveling "The Road to God" has led me to discover that the church, religion, and God can't be judged by what people have defined them to be. There's a line from "The Singer" by Calvin Miller that goes, "Humanity is fickle. They may dress for a morning coronation and never feel the need to change clothes to attend an execution in the afternoon." I discovered it wasn't the church, religion, or God that I was disillusioned with; it was *people*.

People will deceive you, fail you, and let you down. To find God's true church, one must look beyond the brick and mortar of buildings, the ritual and ceremony of man-made worship, and the hypocrisy of people "playing" church, and focus on the grace of God and the love of Jesus Christ.

Where the road to God may lead depends upon one's diligence in seeking the truth, for *"and the truth shall make you free* (John 8:32 KJV)."

It may lead to God and eternal life, or it may lead to death. The following poems offer some reflections on God's love and judgment.

Who Crucified Jesus?

Who crucified Jesus and hung him on the cross,
To be executed and to count his life as lost?
It was a man called Pilate who had the final say;
He yielded to the mob, condemned him on that day.

Who crucified Jesus and nailed him to a tree,
Iron spikes in hands and feet to suffer agony?
It was the Roman soldiers; they're guilty of the deed,
They beat, scourged, and mocked him, and hung him there to bleed.

Who crucified Jesus there on Golgotha's hill,
To be taunted, mocked, and ridiculed, so mercilessly killed?
It was the Jewish leaders, Chief Priests and Pharisees,
Who conspired against him; to his death they agreed.

Who crucified Jesus the Savior and the Christ?
Who gave his life to pay the price that would suffice?
Look into some mirror, the mirror it knows who,
The one for whom he died is looking back at you!

"[5]But he was wounded for our transgressions; he was bruised for our iniquities: the chastisement of our peace was upon him; and with his stripes we are healed."
Isaiah 53:5 (NKJV)

The Minstrel

He was new to these parts, I remember him well,
A minstrel whose lyrics a new story did tell.
He was just passing through, the leader of a band,
Out spreading his message playing one-night stands.

Hair down to his shoulders and sandals on his feet,
A soft smile touched his face, with gentle voice did speak.
Now the boys in the band, they were a motley crew,
They could lay down some licks, play music sweet and true.

His fan base was growing on the farms and in towns,
Number one on the charts, now a group of renown.
His songs stirred people's souls, gave them hope, taught them love,
Their spirits were lifted, brought blessings from above.

Not all liked the music; this new sound hurt their ears,
The new words pierced their souls and aroused their worst fears.
If people kept listening, the old songs wouldn't sell,
So they schemed and plotted; their hearts were made in hell.

Under cover of night they took the minstrel from town,
Where they cursed and beat him and then shot the Minstrel down.
The foul deed was concealed; all the leaders kept quiet,
But there will come a day when all wrongs are made right.

But the music's not dead; it's bigger than ever,
Their plan to defeat him not really so clever.
Minstrel said that he'd leave, but if you'd sing his song,
Some day you could join him 'cause that's where you'd belong.

Yeah, I remember him well, though he didn't stay long,
Had a real catchy tune that Minstrel and his song.
Lots of folks still sing it, so the words must be true,
Things ain't been the same here; I've been singing them too.

". . . the grass withers, and the flower falls, but the word of the Lord endures forever."
1 Peter 1:24-25(NRSV)

Nails of Love

When Jesus gave His life and counted it as loss,
It wasn't three iron nails that held Him to the cross.
From Hades' lowest pit to Heaven's highest hill,
No power could hold Him there against His own will.

Praying in the garden there at Gethsemane,
He had visions of a man, a man who looked like me.
"So if this cup can't pass then in your will I'll stay,
To go and save this man and do it in your way."

As the soldiers scourged Him, His thoughts there were of you:
"If I don't do this thing what on earth will he do?
For him I'll strike a deal with our vile, evil foe,
Eternal life for man for three days down below."

He left Heaven's grandeur, answered the Father's call,
To unveil God's plan to prevent mankind's fall.
Justice could be dispensed to a sinful human race,
But brought them forgiveness through His amazing grace.

It wasn't an iron nail that held one hand to the tree,
It was all Jesus' love that He had just for me.
It wasn't an iron nail that held the other hand too,
It was all Jesus' love that He had just for you.

It wasn't an iron nail holding His feet to the cross,
It was all Jesus' love for the least, last, and lost.
At the old rugged cross of His gift now avails,
The power of nails of love is greater than iron nails.

"For God so loved the world that he gave his only Son, so that everyone who believes in him may not perish but may have eternal life."
John 3:16 (NRSV)

God's Gift to Man

Born in a lowly manger on a night starlit grand,
Let glad hosannas ring for God's gift to man.
As a human God came; Jesus was His name,
Because He came and lived, this world is not the same.

Growing wise through the years lead by His father's hand,
A carpenter by trade, He lived like mortal man.
One day in the temple His purpose revealed clear,
Was time to be about His father's business here.

With a band that followed, they numbered ten and two,
They told of the Good News to Jew and Gentile too.
A message plain and simple, a child could understand,
Of a promised Messiah to be God's gift to man.

Healing blind, raising dead, miracles did perform,
He was the Creator, He even calmed the storms.
All races, creeds, colors, no one would be ignored,
To those who would believe, He said, "Go, and sin no more."

But the leaders feared Him; they wished that He were dead.
They hung Him on a cross with thorns upon His head.
When He cried "It's finished!" with one last gasp of breath,
They could not understand His victory in death.

In three days at the tomb they found an open door;
Man's greatest enemy was His forever more.
In awe of those who watched, He rose to heavenly home,
To intercede for all from His place at God's throne.

So complex by design, yet so simple to be true,
Especially when you think, He did it all for you.
Man's mind can't comprehend God's great redemption plan,
They must by faith believe in God's gift to man.

"For by grace you have been saved through faith, and this is not your own doing; it is the gift of God."
Ephesians 2:8 (NRSV)

The Greatest Miracle

While walking down a hot and dusty road one day,
A traveler stopped to rest in the shade by the way,
Where sat an old man who with greetings wished him well,
Asked him to listen to a story he could tell.

"I'm called Bartimaeus, I was blind and couldn't see,
But then I met a man called Jesus of Galilee.
"Thy faith has made thee whole!" this Jesus said to me;
What happened was a miracle for now my eyes can see."

Later on his journey the traveler saw a crowd,
Gathered around a man speaking with voice loud,
Relating some event to those from far and near.
The traveler moved closer, this story he did hear:

"My name is Lazarus, I just came from the grave,
My tomb was closed and sealed; to death four days a slave.
Then a man called Jesus said, "Lazarus come forth!"
What happened was a miracle, my life had been restored."

Then he met a woman, her face was all aglow,
Helping poor and needy, God's love to others show.
When asked why she had joy, she replied with a sigh,
"It's no secret, traveler, I'll gladly tell you why.

A woman of the streets, I'd lived a life of sin,
My world just shattered dreams, despair I felt within.
Then Jesus touched my life, said, "Go, and sin no more!"
What happened was a miracle for now I've been reborn."

Jesus performed miracles, restored sight, did good deeds,
Raised the dead back to life and He filled many needs.
But when a life and soul is redeemed from sin's pall,
There's no doubt that this is the greatest miracle of all.

"Therefore, if anyone is in Christ, he is a new creation; old things have passed away; behold, all things have become new."
2 Corinthians 5:17 (NKJV)

Because of the Choice He Made

Alone in the garden on a dark fateful night,
He pondered his purpose 'til the break of dawn's light.
"Could this cup pass away?" for an answer He prayed,
To do the Father's will was the choice that He made.

There are things in this life in which I had no choice,
Skin color, tall or short, family name, sound of voice.
But when life's path may end, of my fate not afraid,
For I now have a choice because of the choice He made.

Died with thieves on a hill whose name history knows,
Innocence he could claim, no crime's debt that He owed.
Bands of angels could call, or in a tomb be laid?
Three days in the latter was the choice that He made.

Life is the sum total of choices that you make,
And of all the chances that you do or don't take.
As for a life beyond there has a price been paid,
For you now have a choice because of the choice He made.

" . . . choose this day whom you will serve . . . but as for me and my household, we will serve the Lord."
Joshua 24:15 (NRS)

Sing Me the Story

It was at a tent revival on a starry summer night,
With his hand the Lord "He Touched Me," it was then "I Saw The Light."
That's the reason God's son Jesus hung on "The Old Rugged Cross,"
To bring the world "Amazing Grace" and save people who are lost.

No place "Could I Go" but to where "There's Room At The Cross For You."
He said, "You'll Never Walk Alone" and come "Just As I Am" too.
And so there I knelt "At The Cross," it was a "Sweet Hour of Prayer;"
In tears I prayed "Search Me O God" for "I Need Thee Every Hour."

I chose to "Reach Out To Jesus," "I Was Sinking Deep In Sin,"
"Love Lifted Me" to "Higher Ground" and it gave me peace within.
Now I have "Blessed Assurance" that "It Is Well With My Soul,"
In "Rock Of Ages," "Hide Thou Me," "The Half Has Never Been Told."

Oh, "I Love To Tell The Story" about "This Little Light Of Mine,"
How "He Lives" and "How Great Thou Art" and "He Holds His Hand In Mine."
Yes, those "Precious Memories" get "Sweeter As The Days Go By,"
"I Will Ever Sing Thy Praises" as "Angels We Have Heard On High."

"Sing to the Lord, all the earth; Proclaim the good news of His salvation from day to day."
1 Chronicles 16:23 (NKJV)

When I Pray

You know sometimes dear God when I bow down to pray,
My heart is so heavy I know not what to say.
From silent, trembling lips, I hope that you will hear,
That you can understand the language of my tears.

Lord, sometimes when I pray, my thoughts are all in spin,
Tired in mind and body, troubled of soul within.
The words I cannot speak, I trust you know my groans,
Dear savior of my soul, creator of my bones.

Lord, sometimes when I pray, my world's come crashing down,
I know not where to turn, where answers can be found.
What plan is for my life, you understand my need?
On what path I should go, oh Lord, I pray you'll lead.

Lord, sometimes when I pray, it's words you've heard before,
Just giving you the "thanks" and asking you for more.
Like a broken record it sounds on my part;
Look past these mortal lips and know what's in my heart.

You know, God, I don't know exactly how to pray,
It seems to come out wrong in my plain, simple way.
But, for the chance to talk to a big God like thee,
Well, that's quite an honor for a little man like me.

"For we do not know what we should pray for as we ought, but the Spirit Himself makes intercession for us with groanings which cannot be uttered."
Romans 8:26 (NKJV)

More than Just Words

Lord, I know I've not been true to the promise that I made,
In this way support the church, I have not faithfully prayed.
I'll make a greater effort to lift up the ones who lead,
And seek your help and guidance to help meet your people's needs.

Lord, I know I committed to support it with my presence,
Not putting forth the effort, no excuse for my absence.
I want to be connected to my church family and friends,
I'm going to be more faithful Sunday service to attend.

Lord, I know that I've been slack putting my pledge in the plate,
Been so many bills to pay, thought the church's tithe could wait.
You know my heart and circumstance; I trust you'll fairly judge it,
But I'll try and do my best to give more to the budget.

Lord, I know that I promised I'd be true when service called,
I've been selfish with my time; have not been involved at all.
I want this to be "my" church, to say "we" instead of "they,"
So, help me to find the place you want me to serve today.

Lord, when I joined this, your church, I took a holy vow;
To the promise that I made I make a re-commitment now.
Make these things real in my heart; let them be *more* than just words,
So to better serve and keep this confession you have heard.

[2] "Do not be conformed to this world, but be transformed by the renewing of your minds, so that you may discern what is the will of God—what is good and acceptable and perfect." Romans 12:23 (NRSV)

Judgment

There's many kinds of people in this 'ole world;
Some are in the dark, some have seen the light.
There's coming a day they'll be set apart,
Some on the left, some on the right.

Some are lovers, some are haters,
Some are givers, others takers.
There are forgivers, there are forsakers,
Some true-to-lifers and some just fakers.

Some are searchers, some are preachers,
Some are listeners, others teachers.
There are followers and there are leaders,
Some of them shunners while some are greeters.

Some confessors, some deniers,
Some truth-tellers, others liars.
There are revealers, there are concealers,
Some unrepentant but some believers.

Some are concerned, some indifferent,
Some are helpful, others distant.
There are oppressors, there are defenders,
Some among saints, some among sinners.

There's many kinds of people in this 'ole world,
Some are in the dark, some have seen the light.
There's coming a day they'll be set apart,
Some on the left, some on the right.

"All the nations will be gathered before Him, and He will separate them one from another, as a shepherd divides his sheep from the goats. And He will set the sheep on His right hand, but the goats on the left."
Matthew 25:31-33 (NKJV)

The Lion of Judah

As a babe in a manger He came the first time,
To sounds of celebration and the ringing of chimes.
As a Suffering Servant brought salvation from above,
Taught helping one another, spread a message of love.

But different it will be the second time around,
When the Lion of Judah comes rolling into town.
With four horsemen at His side He will enforce God's wrath,
Visit judgment on the earth, trample foes in His path.

On His order seven angels will trumpets blow in hand,
Pestilence, plagues and fire will spew forth on the land.
The earth to its foundations will shake, stagger, and groan,
Hell and ruin will be unleashed like the world's never known.

Wielding sickle of harvest the Son will reap His own,
With slashing blades of vengeance will cut down the unknown.
The dragon and his legions condemned to fiery lake,
Followed by all the millions who did the Christ forsake.

For those who think Jesus to be a pacifist,
Then will see His other side when He puts down His fist.
When this thing's gone long enough, announces time no more,
And ushers in peace-on-earth with a Word and a Sword.

"The wolf also shall dwell with the lamb,
The leopard shall lie down with the young goat,
The calf and the young lion and the fatling together;
And a little child shall lead them." Isaiah 11:6 (NKJV)

Imagine That!

Imagine a place where there is no sun,
And in darkness of night no moon has been hung.
Where a blue sky at noon will never be seen,
And a star-studded night is only a dream.

Imagine a place where no meadows lie,
No fox and deer roam, no birds in the sky.
The green forests unknown and gardens don't grow,
Where a cool mountain stream is not seen to flow.

Imagine a place with no children at play,
No picnics or road trips or holidays gay.
A place where there's never heard laughter or cheer,
No ease from the suffering, no one to dry tears.
Imagine that!

Imagine a place reigned over by night,
Good can't live in a place that's void of light.
And beauty can't grow in its ugliness,
Righteousness is subdued by its evilness.

Imagine a place that grants no return,
To go back and change time, the clock's hands can't turn.
Where weighed and found wanting for the choice one made,
The cost for a life lived, a debt to be paid.

Imagine a place where Heaven's in view,
But to enter its gates, no access into.
For rejecting God's gift, here one must remain,

For eternity serve in Satan's domain.
Imagine that!

"And cast the unprofitable servant into the outer darkness. There will be weeping and gnashing of teeth."
Matthew 25:30 (NKJV)

CHAPTER 7

Roads Yet Traveled

WHEN OUR SON WAS A JUNIOR in high school, he suddenly collapsed following one of his high school team's soccer games. X-rays revealed an enlarged lymph node in his chest. After ensuing tests, the doctors concluded that there was a ninety percent chance our son had lymphoma. Major surgery would be required to biopsy the lymph node in order to make a definite diagnosis. That was a defining moment in our family's lives. One day life is great, and then out of the blue you're hit with the stark reality of, "what does tomorrow hold?"

In the chapter "Back Roads," I referenced the quote, "Yesterday is a memory, tomorrow is a mystery, today is a gift." We make plans for what roads we're going to travel tomorrow, next week, next month, and next year, but we really don't know what "roads yet traveled" lie unknown before us. Tomorrow is a mystery, a black hole, and we have no way of knowing what fortunes or misfortunes it may hold. We had no idea that day what kinds of roads we were going to have to travel in those coming weeks and months.

The evening before the day our son was to have surgery, I was sitting on our living room couch nervously thumbing through a magazine when I heard a voice say, "don't worry, everything's going to be okay." Speechless, I paused and looked around for a moment. My wife and son, who were also in the room, didn't hear the voice but it was as audible to me as if one of them had spoken. In that moment, a peace settled over me that I can't find words to describe.

The following morning as we prepared to leave for the hospital, these words from a hymn were going around and around in my head: "To God be the glory, great things he hath done!" After several hours of surgery, the surgeon came out and explained to us that the surgery had gone well and that he saw no signs of any cancer. In fact, the doctors could not explain what had caused the lymph node to enlarge; whatever had been there was gone! To God be the glory!

As I contemplate what roads are waiting out there yet to be traveled, hopefully there will be several more miles on the "Roads of Time" and a few more trips wandering "Back Roads." There may be another "Road of No Return" or two to face, and still some stops to ponder on the "The Lost Highway." I must also anticipate there'll be some roads to be traveled that I don't even know about. But, wherever my "Roads Yet Traveled" may lead, there are two things I've learned from my journey this far: I'll continue on "The Road to God," for I know "I Never Walk Alone."

We can't know where our "Roads Yet Traveled" may lead, because life doesn't always turn out the way we plan. The following poems offer hope and assurance for the roads yet traveled.

I Never Walk Alone

Through the Valley of Death I have walked without rest,
Climbed the snow-capped mountain, seen the world from its crest.
Traversed parched desert sands where the hot winds have blown,
But wherever I've walked, I've never walked alone.

I have walked in the cold 'til chilled through to the bone,
In the hot, baking sun walked through fields of sharp stone.
Through the wet, soaking rain along roads I have roamed,
But wherever I've walked, I've never walked alone.

In the cities and towns wandered streets of all names,
I've strolled along highways and serene country lanes.
Hiked many long pathways through jungles overgrown,
But wherever I've walked, I've never walked alone.

I have ventured new roads marked with hills and dead ends,
Traveled on old byways filled with ruts and sharp bends.
Journeyed on pathways that to the Four Winds has blown,
But wherever I've walked, I've never walked alone.

What roads yet un-traveled do lie waiting for me?
On what course they may take, mortal eyes cannot see.
Yet, I walk without fear; I'll be not on my own,
Wherever roads may lead, I never walk alone.

Psalm 23 (Revised)

I know the Lord is my shepherd, His ways I don't understand,
Winds of change sweep o'er His people, spread confusion in the land.
Beyond bounds of ease and comfort, no promise of want or need,
Be it the work of God or man, who doth truly take the lead?

He makes me to lie down in fields where the ground is parched and dry,
I wonder why I'm in this place, then I stop and question why.
He leads beside troubled waters; the storms toss my ship about,
I'm unsure of my direction and my heart is filled with doubt.

Will He now restore my soul, renew my strength in due time?
Mount me up on wings of eagles to top the mountain that I climb?
He leads on the narrow pathways where roots and rocks trip my way,
Stumbling, falling, and discouraged, from the path hard not to stray.

I walk the lonely, dark valley as if Death's presence is near,
Coming days hold the unknown, the midnight hour innate fear.
The rod and staff give comfort only when the shepherd's near,
To a lonely wandering traveler, the master's voice faint of ear.

He sets a table before me but its spread seems meager fare,
To sustain me for the battle in the world I face out there.
For the enemies are many, they attack from every side,
I am but a single person; I can't alone stem the tide.

I am more the Prodigal than the blessed anointed one;
Sell the oil for use on the poor, waste not on a doubting son.
I pray that my cup will be filled so for my soul's thirst to quell,
But the elixir eludes me, much like the famed Holy Grail.

Surely more evil will follow in end-of-days the earth defile;
What portent doth the Book betray, what fate for destiny's child?
When things of earth are on the pyre, victim of angelic sword,
No more this earthly life of woe, but peace in the House of the Lord.

Because He's a divine shepherd, I can't always know His way,
For I am but a mere mortal, just a man of dust and clay.
But He is my only shepherd and wherever He may lead,
Because He is the Good Shepherd, I trust Him to meet my need.

To Sense God

I see Him in a seed that hides the great oak tree,
In the face of someone whose soul has been set free.
I see Him in a cross upon the alter stand,
In a tattered old coat concealing needy hands.

I hear Him in the cry of new life being born,
In a still small voice when I'm weary and worn.
I hear Him in songbirds and in the stormy wind,
In a Sunday sermon calling me from my sin.

I smell Him in meadows of spring's fragrant delights,
On mom's leather Bible she read to me at night.
I smell Him in candles on holy Christmas Eves,
On the breath of a drunk who needs help to believe.

I taste Him in the rain of a summer rain cloud,
In the bread and the juice there on bended knee bowed.
I taste Him at a table with my friends breaking bread,
In the warm tears of joy when a loved one is wed.

I feel Him in nature, His divine glory shown,
In His spirit that leads and makes my pathways known.
I feel Him in a choir singing Amazing Grace,
At a solemn graveside at the end of a race.

At Times . . .

At times my spirit does take flight as a bird on the wing,
To break loose from bounds of earth to realms where angels sing.
As wind beneath eagle's wings lifts it from valley floor,
To the lofty mountain heights, above its peaks to soar.

At times my soul does find peace in the hush of the night,
When a still, small voice whispers in the dark calm and quiet.
As in a wood autumn leaves in gentle breeze do sway,
Stir long forgotten memories and fond times of bygone days.

At times my mind is as bright as a shiny diamond stone,
To see things before unseen, know things before unknown.
As in a glass darkly seen, made to see face-to-face,
To be known as one is known and find each one his place.

At times my heart brims with joy as waterfalls cascade,
For the wondrous things of life and answers to prayers prayed.
As I seek my Holy Grail, a presence fills my space;
It stirs my soul to reflect and sense amazing grace.

Weep Not For Me

I know you weep for I am gone,
Soon to be laid beneath the stone.
You gather 'round to bid me peace,
Through tears of grief to seek release.

But let your grief be spared for me,
For from this world I've been set free.
Mourn for yourself you prison-bound,
In mortal flesh with suffering crowned.

Gone? No, not gone! That, don't believe,
Now in a place that eye can't see.
Done left behind a house of clay,
A new one waits that God has made.

Someday when your earth's work is done,
Eternity's prize has been won.
Together we'll forever stay,
Where tears from eyes are wiped away.

THE END

About the Author

G.W. Scott grew up in rural areas and small towns in East Tennessee near an entrance to the Great Smoky Mountains. With a degree in computer science from the University of Tennessee, Scott enjoyed a long career as a computing analyst in the business, aircraft, and government arenas. Scott enjoys writing, teaching, and speaking and is an experienced training instructor, Sunday school teacher, and presenter at technical conferences. *The Betrayal of Lincoln Crockett*, his second foray into the wide world of literature, is an exciting drama, action, and mystery novel. Now retired, Scott and his wife Peggy make their home in Lenoir City, Tennessee.

Other work by G.W. Scott

Lincoln Crockett is a young man troubled of mind and soul and seeking to come to grips with the "whys" of the world that, left unresolved, leave him with an unexplained feeling of emptiness, a void somewhere deep inside. He is on a quest for truth and redemption. This quest takes him on an unimaginable journey that runs the full gamut of human emotions. Ride along with Lincoln as he experiences drama, adventure, and comedy. You will share the tears, feel the heartbreak, empathize with the loss, taste the anger, and chuckle at the humor as he strives against centuries-old social forces of prejudice and class systems to find peace. Meet colorful characters and marvel at the secrets they harbor, the agendas they pursue, and the mischief they stir. A sexy hotel manager, gangsters, bootleggers, a crooked sheriff, a jackleg preacher, a fancy carnival owner, a federal agent, a half-wit ferry operator, a brave best friend, and a southern beauty fill the pages with excitement as Lincoln gets entangled in an assortment of misadventures. Experience the Moonshine War; listen in on Lincoln's conversation with his dead parents; observe the heated constitutional debate between Lincoln and the sheriff; pin your ears back for Reverend Nutter's fiery sermons. Does Lincoln find the truth? Does he reconcile the "whys?" Does he find redemption? There's only one way to find out.

Available on Amazon.com, Barnesandnoble.com, on Kindle, and from select retailers.

Made in United States
Orlando, FL
08 January 2024

42241677R00057